INDIGENOUS AMERICAN CULTURES

Celebrating the CHOCTAW

KIM THOMPSON

Mitchell Lane
PUBLISHERS

Parent and Caregiver Tips for Creating Nonfiction Readers

The high-interest topics in the ***Indigenous American Cultures*** series are sure to get your young reader excited about reading nonfiction. While exploring a fascinating subject, your reader will be introduced to new facts, ideas, and vocabulary.

Tips for Reading Nonfiction

Talk about Nonfiction

Explain that nonfiction books provide facts about real-world topics. When readers read nonfiction, they gain a rich understanding of the world. They build background knowledge that provides a foundation for learning and academic success.

Look at the Parts

This book contains the following helpful features. Share the purpose of each feature with your reader.

Photos, Captions, and Graphic Aids
The photos, captions, maps, diagrams, time lines, and other graphic aids in nonfiction texts contain a wealth of information. Help your reader identify different ways information can be displayed.

Sidebars
These extra tidbits of information help satisfy readers' curiosity and expand their knowledge.

Table of Contents
Located at the front of the book, this list shows the big ideas within the text and the page numbers where they can be found.

Glossary
Located at the back of the book, the glossary defines key words and phrases that are related to the topic. These words and phrases can be found in the text in colored type.

Comprehension Questions (Fact Check)
Multiple-choice questions help readers self-check to make sure they understand what they read.

Index
Located at the back of the book, the index is an alphabetical list of topics and the page numbers where they can be found.

With a little help and guidance, your reader will be on their way to enjoying and learning from nonfiction books.

Mitchell Lane
PUBLISHERS
mitchelllanepub.com

2001 SW 31st Avenue
Hallandale, FL 33009

First Edition, 2027.
Author: Kim Thompson
Designer: Rhea Magaro

Series: Indigenous American Cultures
Title: Celebrating the Choctaw / by Kim Thompson

Hallandale, FL : Mitchell Lane Publishers, [2027]

Library bound ISBN: 979-8-89260-916-6
Paperback ISBN: 979-8-90145-067-3
eBook ISBN: 979-8-90145-026-0

Library of Congress
Control Number: 2026930180

PHOTO CREDITS
Alamy: PA Images, 1; North Wind Picture Archives, 5; Rick Lewis, 5; The Picture Art Collection, 6; Florilegius, 7; GemStocks, 9; PA Images, 13, 14; Zip Lexing, 15; Danita Delimont, 19; J Marshall - Tribaleye Images, 20; Imago, 21; Nature and Science, 23, 28; ZUMA Press, Inc., 25; Dreamstime: Fckncg, 1; Public Domain: Wikipedia, 8, 13, 18, 26, 27; choctawnation, 11, 17, 24, 27; Library of Congress, 16; National Gallery of Art, 22; Shutterstock: Gr8t Shots, 1; Silvio Ligutti, 1; Svitlana_ Shepitsena, 9; 365 Focus Photography, 12; wjarek, 21; Leon Brezer, 26; Carmen K. Sisson, 29;

CONTENTS

A CHOCTAW CONNECTION

Have you ever visited a farmers market? Did you see stacks of fresh-picked vegetables and other foods?

In the early 1700s, there weren't many places in North America to shop for food. One place was a busy market near the Mobile River in present-day Alabama. French **settlers** came here to trade for food raised by the Choctaw. At that time, these **Indigenous** people lived across land that became Mississippi, Alabama, and Louisiana.

The Choctaw were expert farmers. They grew corn, beans, pumpkins, sunflowers, and more. Their methods were so advanced that they often had extra food. This allowed them to trade with Europeans and with other tribes.

Culture Close-Up

The Choctaw cleared land for farming and for raising cattle. To do it, they **girdled** trees. They burned tree stumps and roots to enrich the soil.

CHOCTAW HISTORY

Choctaw history in North America goes back thousands of years. The tribe is related to the ancient Mound Builders who once lived in large cities near the Mississippi River.

Long ago, the Choctaw built homes of logs plastered with mud. Women led households and farmed. Men hunted and protected the tribe.

Every Choctaw belonged to a **clan**. Children joined their mother's clan. Villages were divided into three districts. A male chief led each district.

Culture Close-Up

Before a Choctaw funeral, the body was raised on a platform high in the trees.

The United States government pressured the Choctaw to sign **treaties** and give up their vast lands. Beginning in 1831, soldiers forced about 15,000 Choctaw to walk west to "Indian Territory" that later became Oklahoma. This terrible journey is known as the Trail of Tears. Thousands of Choctaw died on the way.

In Oklahoma, the Choctaw Nation reformed its government. Today, it has over 225,000 members. Many live on the nation's **reservation**.

Some Choctaw remained in their homelands. Their **descendants** form the Mississippi Band of Choctaw Indians and the Jena Band of Choctaw Indians in Louisiana.

Culture Close-Up

White settlers called the Choctaw, Chickasaw, Cherokee, Muscogee, and Seminole the "Five Civilized Tribes." These tribes traded with Americans and adopted their ways. All were forced to give up their land and walk the Trail of Tears.

EXPLORING CHOCTAW PLACES

To learn about the Choctaw, you can visit an earth mound in Winston County, Mississippi. It was built by people about 2,000 years ago.

The Choctaw call it *Nanih Waiya* or Mother Mound. A legend says the first people emerged from a cave nearby. They gathered on the mound. Some left to form different tribes. Choctaw people decided to stay.

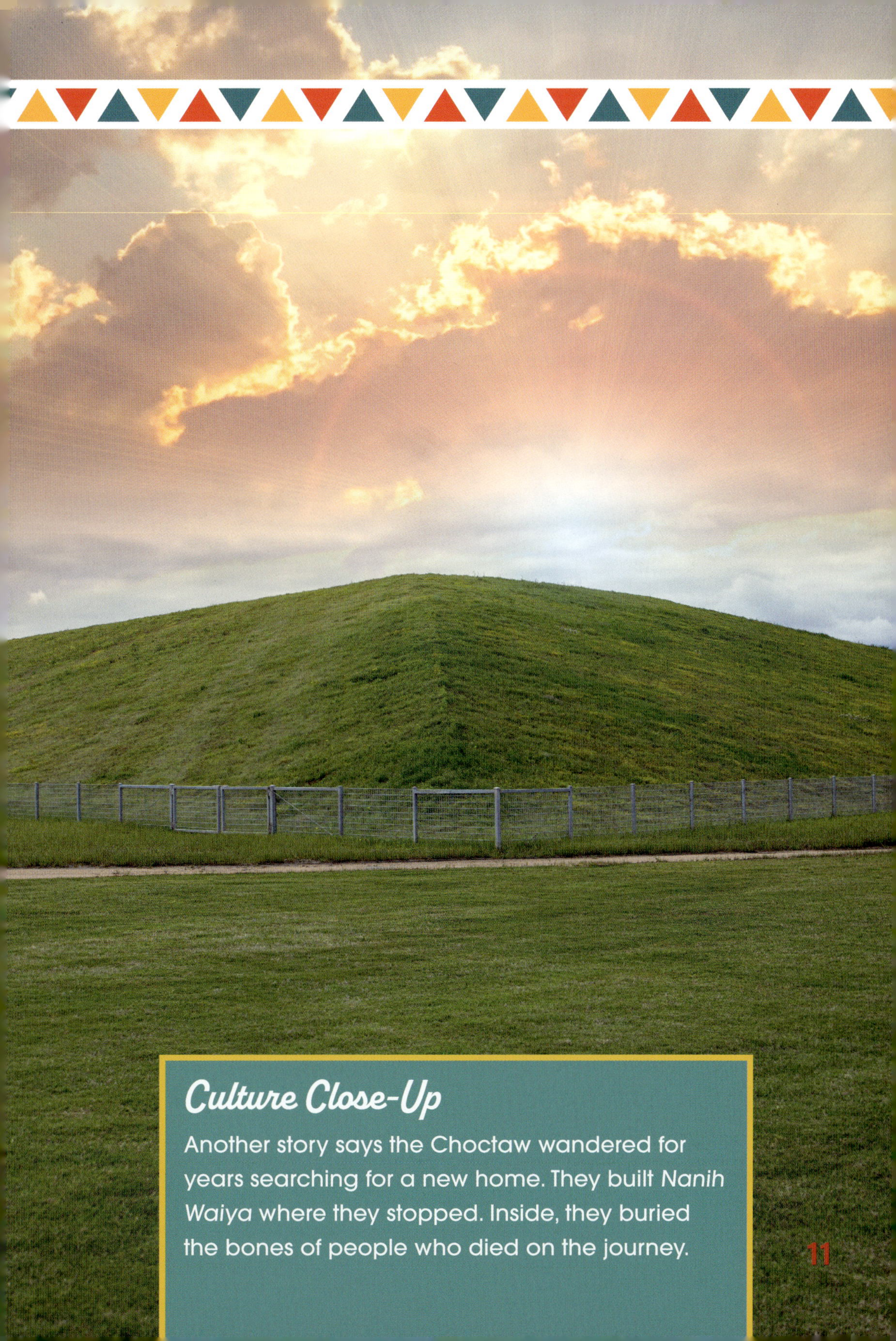

Culture Close-Up

Another story says the Choctaw wandered for years searching for a new home. They built *Nanih Waiya* where they stopped. Inside, they buried the bones of people who died on the journey.

You can visit a park in County Cork, Ireland, to see *Kindred Spirits* by Alex Pentek. The sculpture shows eagle feathers in the shape of a food bowl. Traditionally, the Choctaw give eagle feathers as a reward for great deeds.

In 1847, Choctaw people were still suffering from the Trail of Tears. Many were poor and hungry. They learned about the **Great Famine** happening in Ireland. They felt great sympathy for the Irish people. To help, the tribe donated the little money they had. Years later, the sculpture was made to honor the Choctaw's kindness.

During the Great Famine, many Irish families starved.

Culture Close-Up

The Irish and Choctaw continue to have a special friendship. In 2018, Irish leader Leo Varadkar visited the Choctaw Nation. He announced a scholarship program to help Choctaw students study in Ireland.

THE CHOCTAW LANGUAGE

The Choctaw language is part of the Muskogean language family. It was written down much earlier than other Indigenous languages. By the 1830s, Choctaw children used books to help them learn their language. Today, Choctaw is spoken widely in the tribe.

Culture Close-Up

The Choctaw call themselves *Chahta*. The name may come from an ancient Choctaw leader. It may come from the phrase *hacha hatak*, which means "river people."

Culture Close-Up

Practice these Choctaw words and phrases.

Chi pisa la chike. (See you later.)

Chukkowa. (Come in.)

Haklo! (Listen!)

Halito! (Hello!)

Yakoke. (Thank you.)

Choctaw soldiers used their language to send secret messages in World War I. These Code Talkers helped the U.S. win many battles.

HONORING CHOCTAW TRADITIONS

Long ago, the Choctaw played stickball to settle disputes. The full-contact, lacrosse-like sport was used in place of war with other tribes. It helped warriors stay in shape. It taught hand-eye coordination skills that were important for hunting.

Choctaw people still enjoy stickball. Some use wood and leather to craft traditional sticks and balls. The game is played in tournaments and during celebrations. Men's and women's teams play in the World Series of Stickball.

The Choctaw believe that eagles take messages to the Creator. The Eagle Dance asks for rain, victory in battle, and other blessings. Dancers wear eagle feathers and move like eagles.

Long ago, the War Dance helped warriors prepare for battle. Men danced in a circle around the women. Other traditional Choctaw dances mimicked animals. The Turtle Dance asked for long life. The Raccoon Dance invited playfulness.

After the Choctaw were sent to Oklahoma, their dances nearly died out. But tribal elders remembered, and they taught young people. Today, social dancing is a popular way for Choctaw people to meet and celebrate.

Culture Close-Up

Ancient Choctaw wore animal skins and cloth woven from plants. Modern traditional Choctaw styles began in the 1700s. Men wear brightly colored cotton shirts and black hats. Women wear long dresses. Ribbons, beads, and ruffles are used for decoration.

Long ago, the Choctaw carved beads from shells. Later, they traded with Europeans for glass beads. Diamonds in their intricate bead designs represented the Eastern diamondback rattlesnake.

Ancient Choctaw dug clay to make pots. They wove river cane to make beautiful and useful baskets. These containers were important for carrying trade goods.

Jeffrey Gibson

Today, Choctaw artists continue these traditions. Jeffrey Gibson is a painter and sculptor. He includes Choctaw designs and themes in his work. He uses colorful beads in surprising ways.

CHOCTAW CELEBRATIONS

The Green Corn Ceremony is traditionally celebrated in midsummer when the first corn is ripe. For the Choctaw, it is a time of feasting, dancing, and forgiveness.

This old ritual is the origin of today's Choctaw Indian Fair. The fair is hosted each July by the Mississippi Band of Choctaw Indians. It includes art, dancing, stickball, and traditional foods.

Culture Close-Up

Hominy is made from corn dried in the husk. It simmers for hours over an open fire. With meat and beans, it makes a hearty stew.

One of the largest **powwows** in the U.S. is the Choctaw Powwow. It is held each autumn at the Choctaw Cultural Center in Durant, Oklahoma. Indigenous people from all over the nation come to dance, sing, drum, and compete for prizes. The Choctaw War Dance is a featured event.

The Choctaw Cultural Center has educational exhibits, a living history village, and a stickball field.

FAMOUS FACES

Chief Pushmataha led Choctaw soldiers who fought for the U.S. in the War of 1812. He stood up to government officials to protect Choctaw land. He is buried in Washington, D.C.

Chief Pushmataha

Culture Close-Up

Former NFL quarterback Brett Favre is Choctaw on his father's side.

Gary Dale Batton

Gary Dale Batton is the current chief of the Choctaw Nation of Oklahoma. It is the third-largest tribe in the U.S.

Ada Brown

Ada Brown is a U.S. district judge. She was appointed in 2019 by President Donald Trump. She is a member of the Choctaw Nation of Oklahoma.

LESSONS FROM THE CHOCTAW

The Choctaw are **resilient**. They have overcome many hardships. They have survived as a strong people who have made great contributions to America.

Modern Choctaw people lead ordinary modern lives. But they remember their past and celebrate their culture. Their traditions teach important lessons about the power of community.

GLOSSARY

clan (klan): a small group of people within a tribe; a group of people descended from a common ancestor

descendants (di-SEN-duhnts): your children, their children, and so on into the future; people descended from an ancestor

girdled (GER-duhld): cut a ring of bark from a tree to make the tree die because water and nutrients cannot flow up its trunk

Great Famine (grayt FAM-in): a period from 1845 to 1852 when a disease destroyed potato crops in Ireland, causing one out of every eight people to die of starvation

Indigenous (in-DI-juh-nuhs): the earliest known inhabitants of a place

powwows (POU-wouz): gatherings of Indigenous Americans that are organized for social or ceremonial reasons and that may include traditional singing, dancing, and drumming

reservation (rez-ur-VAY-shuhn): an area of land set aside by the government for ownership by an Indigenous American tribe

resilient (ri-ZIL-yuhnt): able to recover from bad things that happen or to adjust to changes; being strong during tough times

settlers (SET-luhrz): people who make their homes in a new place and who have historically invaded and oppressed Indigenous peoples who originally lived there

treaties (TREE-tees): agreements between two or more groups of people

FACT CHECK

1. Choctaw homelands include land that became __________.
   A. Oklahoma B. Ohio C. Mississippi

2. The Trail of Tears was __________.
   A. a war B. a forced journey C. a treaty

3. Nanih Waiya is __________.
   A. a mound B. a dance C. a kind of pottery

4. Code Talkers used __________ to help win battles.
   A. stickball B. the Choctaw language C. hunting skills

Answers: 1. C, 2. B, 3. A, 4. B

FURTHER READING

Chuculate, Eddie. *This Indian Kid: A Native American Memoir.* Scholastic Focus, 2023.

Hale, E. A. *Indigenous History from 1887–1932: The Allotment and Assimilation Era.* North Star Editions, 2025.

ON THE INTERNET

Choctaw Nation of Oklahoma
choctawnation.com
Explore the official website of one of the largest Indigenous tribes in the United States.

Corn Husk Dolls: How-To
choctawnation.com/wp-content/uploads/2023/07/how-to-corn-husk-doll.pdf
Find directions for making a traditional Choctaw craft.

Powwows.com
powwows.com/webcast/pow-wow-live-streams
Watch a live stream of Indigenous American dancers from around the country.

INDEX

ABOUT THE AUTHOR

Kim Thompson has written more than one hundred books for young readers. She is a fan of American history and loves digging deep to explore stories from the past. Kim thinks it's important to remember ancestors and keep cultural traditions alive. She's grateful for the privilege and adventure of writing this book.